# Quick and Easy
# Quilting Set

## PROJECTS BOOK

**Reader's Digest**

The Reader's Digest Association, Inc.
Pleasantville, New york/Montreal

# CONTENTS

# Introduction

If you've ever longed to make a beautiful quilt but felt that you didn't have the time or the expertise, now is your chance. The Quick and Easy Quilting Set not only offers you a wonderful range of quilt designs in the Projects book but also tells you in the accompanying Techniques book how to create them with maximum ease and speed.

Use the rotary cutter provided in your kit to prepare all of your patches. Piece them on a sewing machine to make blocks and watch your quilt grow. With machine quilting, your quilt will be ready to display proudly.

Projects in this book suit all levels of ability, from the simple Ohio Star block (page 7) that you can make using the fabric in your kit to the more advanced bed-size Memory Quilt (page 81) that features beautiful machine-quilted blocks and borders. Try your hand at a richly colored pillow with an Amish design (page 25) or make a statement with the backpack embellished with panels of flying geese (page 61).

In the following pages, you will also find projects for all the rooms in your home, from the delightful Crib Set (page 51) in pastel colors for the nursery, to the luxurious Shower Curtain (page 67) for the bathroom. Make a pretty Table Mat and Napkin set (page 43) for the dining room or a Maple Leaf Miniature Quilt (page 87) that can be displayed as a table center. Christmas projects in festive prints and metallic fabrics like—the Christmas Table Runner (page 31) and Pinwheel Mantel Cover (page 37), will set your seasonal decorations off to perfection.

*Top: Shower curtain, page 66;*
*Bottom: Memory Quilt, page 81*

## USING THE MEASUREMENTS IN THIS BOOK

When using the books in *The Quick and Easy Quilting Set*, it is important to follow *either* the imperial measurements *or* the metric measurements—don't use a combination of the two. The standard seam allowance for the quilting projects is ¼ in. unless otherwise stated, and the metric equivalent is 0.75 cm.

Each project comes with clear, fully illustrated, step-by-step instructions, enabling you to progress easily through cutting the patches, piecing the blocks, and quilting the projects. Cross-references to the Techniques book are provided at the bottom of the pages where necessary, so you can quickly turn to the relevant section to check up on the basics. Useful tips are provided throughout to give extra information.

So get out your rotary cutting equipment and sewing machine, buy a range of gorgeous fabrics, and start piecing. You'll soon discover why quilting is such a popular craft.

*Christmas Table Runner, page 31*

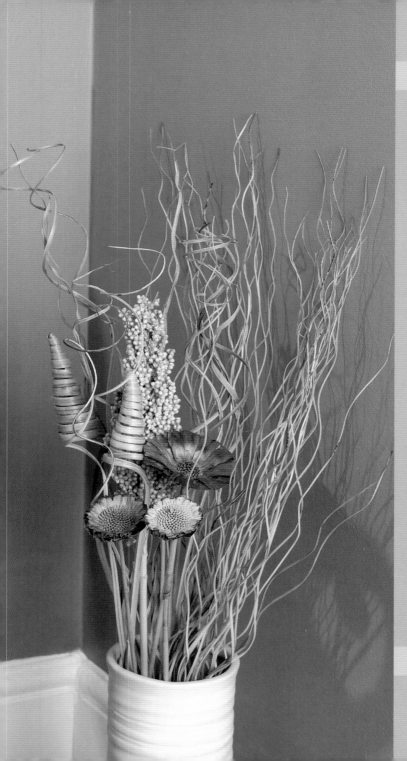

# Ohio Star Block

Use the pretty plaid fabrics supplied in your kit to piece this traditional Ohio Star block design. You can make it as an eye-catching wall hanging with a narrow binding or frame it with a wide border to make a cushion cover. If you make the cushion cover, you will need to buy extra fabric for the border and backing.

The star points are created from quarter-square triangle units, which are easy to assemble using a quick-piecing method.

## Skill Level: Beginner

# Ohio Star
# Wall Hanging

## YOU WILL NEED

**For wall hanging 8¾ x 8¾ in. (22 x 22 cm)**

Fabric from your kit:

- Pink check for star points
- Blue gingham for outer squares and triangles
- Plain green for inner triangles
- Blue-green check for center square
- Plain green for backing and border
- Batting from your kit
- Rotary cutter from your kit
- Quilter's ruler and cutting mat
- Gray cotton thread from your kit
- Two curtain rings and fine cord or narrow ribbon for hanging

## CUTTING LIST

All measurements include ¼-in. (0.75-cm) seam allowances.

**Blue-green check square**

- Use as is. Make sure that the piece is square.

**Pink-check strip**

- Cut into 2 equal squares to match blue-green check above.

**Blue gingham strip**

- Cut into 5 equal squares to match blue-green check above.

**Small plain green square**

- Use as is. Trim to match the blue-green check square.

**Large plain green square**

- Cut square to fit completed pieced block for backing.
- Cut 2 strips 1½ in. (4 cm) wide x height of block, and 2 strips 1½ in. (4 cm) wide x width of block plus two finished binding widths (plus ½ in. (1.5 cm) for turnings) for binding.

Before you begin stitching, measure all your small squares to make sure they are the same size. Trim square if necessary, using your rotary cutter and a quilter's ruler.

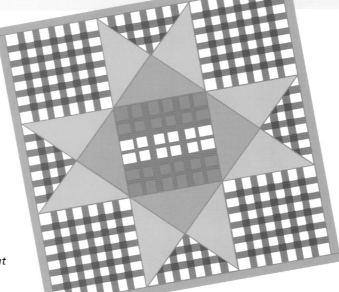

*Wall-hanging layout*

1   Take one pink-check square and one blue gingham square and, using the quick-piecing method on page 27 of the Techniques book, make four quarter-square triangle units. Press the seam allowances toward the darker patches and trim off the "dog ears."

2   From the remaining pink-check square and the small plain green square, make four quarter-square triangle units as in step 1.

3   Lay out the triangle units as shown. Pin them together in pairs with right sides facing, matching the seams carefully. Stitch the diagonal seams. Press the seam allowances toward the darker fabric and trim the "dog ears."

## Seam Allowance

*When hemming or stitching pieces together, always leave a minimum ¼ in. seam allowance.*

See Techniques book, page 27, for quick-piecing quarter-square triangle units.

**4** Using the rotary cutter from your kit and a quilter's ruler, trim the blue-green check square and the remaining four blue gingham squares to match the size of the pieced squares.

**5** Lay out the squares as shown for the Ohio Star block. Pin and stitch them together in three horizontal rows. Press the seam allowances toward the outer edges of the block in the top and bottom rows, and toward the center in the middle row.

## Perfect Points

*When you are stitching two rows together, match the star points by sticking a pin vertically through the point on the top row and straight down through the point on the lower row. Pin the seam on either side in the usual way, then remove the vertical pin.*

**6** Pin and stitch the top row to the middle row, matching seams carefully so that the star points join neatly. Pin and stitch the middle row to the bottom row. Press the seam allowances away from the center row.

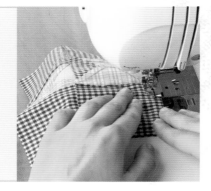

See Techniques book, page 28, for assembling pieced blocks.

7   Trim the batting and backing to match the pieced Ohio Star block. Place the backing wrong side up on your work surface. Lay the batting, then the pieced block right side up on top. Pin the three layers together at intervals across the block.

8   Take the two shorter binding strips and press them in half lengthwise with wrong sides together. Pin them to the sides of the block as shown and stitch. Turn the strips to the wrong side. Press under ¼ in. (0.75 cm) and slip stitch to the backing.

### A Neat Trim

*Once you have pieced your Ohio Star block, it might be necessary to trim the edges to square it up. Place your quilter's ruler on top of the block with one edge lined up with the block edge and trim off any uneven seam endings with a rotary cutter.*

9   Press longer binding strips in half lengthwise and press under ¼ in. (0.75 cm) along each long edge. With right sides facing, turning in raw ends by ¼ in. (0.75 cm), pin and stitch to top and bottom of block. Turn strips to wrong side; slip stitch to backing. Sew two curtain rings to quilt back with fine cord.

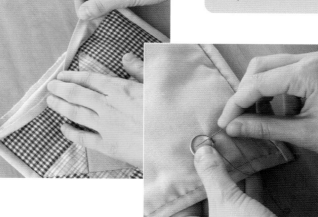

# Ohio Star Cushion

## YOU WILL NEED

**For cushion 15 x 15 in. (38 x 38 cm)**

- Fabric and batting for Ohio Star block—as for hanging
- Cotton fabric backing for block, 10 x 10 in. (25 x 25 cm)
- ¾ yd. (0.7 m) fabric for border and backing
- Gray cotton thread from kit
- Rotary cutter from kit
- Quilter's ruler/cutting mat
- Quilter's safety pins
- Pillow form, 16 x 16 in. (40 x 40 cm)

*Cushion layout*

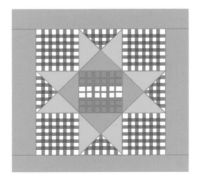

## CUTTING LIST

**Block fabrics**

- Cut as for Ohio Star wall hanging.

**Border fabric**

- For side borders, cut 2 strips 3½ in. (9 cm) wide to fit height of block.
- For top and bottom borders, cut 2 strips 3½ in. (9 cm) wide to fit width of block plus two border widths plus ½ in. (1.5 cm) for seam allowances.
- For cushion back, cut square to fit completed cushion front.

**1** Follow steps 1 to 6 of the Ohio Star wall hanging to piece the block. Layer the block with the batting and cotton backing. Baste the three layers together at regular intervals with quilter's safety pins.

**2** Using the gray cotton thread from your kit, quilt in-the-ditch around the patches in the block. Trim the excess batting and cotton backing to be even with the block edges.

*See* Techniques book, pages 38–42, for quilting information.

3  Pin and stitch the two shorter border strips to the sides of the block. Press the seam allowances toward the border.

## Pressing Borders

*Be careful not to flatten the quilted block when you are pressing the border seams. Keep the bulk of the iron on the border strip and use just the tip to press along the seam.*

4  Trim the two longer border strips to fit the top and bottom edges of the block, including the side borders. Pin and stitch them in place. Press the seam allowances toward the borders.

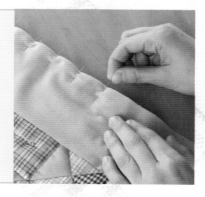

5  Pin the backing fabric to the cushion front with right sides facing. Stitch around the sides and top, leaving the bottom edge open. Clip the corners, and turn right side out. Insert the pillow form and slip stitch the opening closed.

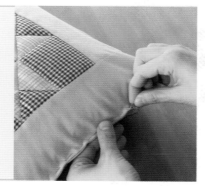

# Nine-Patch Bed Set

Pink roses set off by two shades
of green give this quilt and matching
pillowcase a country feel.
The nine-patch blocks on the quilt are
made from strip sets that are simplicity
itself to sew, cut up, and reassemble.

And there's another chance to make the
Ohio Star wall hanging from Project 1
to coordinate with the set.

Skill Level: Beginner

# Nine-Patch Bed Quilt

## CUTTING LIST

All measurements include ¼-in. (0.75-cm) seam allowances.

**Dark green print**

- o Cut 10 strips 4½ x 42 in. (11.5 x 106 cm).

**Light green print**

- o Cut 8 strips 4½ x 42 in. (11.5 x 106 cm).

**Pink rose print**

- o Cut 5 strips 12½ x 42 in. (31.5 x 106 cm). Cut strips into 15 squares 12½ x 12½ in. (31.5 x 31.5 cm).

**Dark red print**

- o Cut 2 lengthwise strips 5½ in. (14 cm) wide x length of quilt and 2 lengthwise strips 5½ in. (14 cm) wide x width of quilt plus 2 border widths for border.

- o Cut 2 lengthwise pieces 42 x 88 in. (106.5 x 223 cm) for backing.

- o Cut 4 lengthwise strips 3 x 78 in. (7.5 x 198 cm) for binding.

## YOU WILL NEED

**For bed quilt 70 x 82 in. (175 x 205 cm)**

Yardage based on 44-in.- (112-cm-) wide fabric with a usable width of 42 in. (106 cm)

- o 1½ yd. (1.4 m) dark green print for blocks

- o 1¼ yd. (1.2 m) light green print for blocks

- o 2 yd. (1.8 m) pink rose print for blocks

- o 5 yd. (4.6 m) dark red print for borders, backing, and binding

- o Batting, 81 x 96 in. (206 x 244 cm)

- o Rotary cutter, quilter's ruler, and cutting mat

- o Sewing thread

- o Quilter's safety pins

- o Thread for machine quilting

*Bed quilt layout*

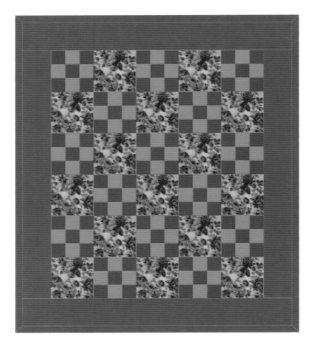

1 To begin making the nine-patch blocks, make a strip set from two dark green print strips and one light green print strip. Repeat to make a total of four strip sets.

## Set Your Seams

*As you add each strip to the strip set, press the seam flat along the stitching line first—this sets the seam. Then open out the strips and press the allowances toward the darker fabric.*

2 Make another strip set from two light green print strips and one dark green print strip. Repeat to make a total of two strip sets.

3 Crosscut the dark/light/dark strip sets into 4½-in. (11.5-cm) segments for a total of 30 units. Crosscut the light/dark/light strip sets into 4½-in. (11.5-cm) segments for a total of 15 units.

*See* Techniques book, page 25, for strip-piecing nine-patch blocks.

**4** Lay out two dark/light/dark units and one light/dark/light unit in three horizontal rows for one nine-patch block. Stitch the units together. Press. Make a total of 15 nine-patch blocks.

## Perfect Corner

*So that the squares in your block meet neatly at the corners, make sure you align the seams of the units accurately when stitching the horizontal rows together.*

**5** Join three nine-patch blocks and two alternate pink rose-print blocks to make one row of the quilt (see bed quilt layout on page 16). Press the seam allowances toward the pink rose-print blocks. Make a total of three rows.

**6** To make the remaining three rows of the quilt, join two nine-patch blocks and three alternate pink rose-print blocks (see bed quilt layout on page 16). Then press the seam allowances toward the pink rose-print blocks.

*See* Techniques book, page 33, for setting blocks.

7 Join all the horizontal rows of blocks together, making sure that the nine-patch blocks and the pink rose-print blocks alternate in checkerboard fashion.

8 Measure the quilt top through the center and cut two 5½-in.- (14-cm-) wide border strips from the dark red-print fabric to fit. Pin and stitch them to the sides of the quilt. Press the seam allowances toward the borders.

## Cut Sharp

*For long border strips, cut along the length of the fabric in several shorter sections. With each new cut, align the ruler with part of the previous cut to keep the fabric edge straight.*

9 Measure the width of the quilt top, including the width of the two border strips. Cut two 5½-in.- (14-cm-) wide border strips from the dark red-print fabric to fit. Pin and stitch them to the quilt top and bottom.

*See* Techniques book, page 35, for making overlapped borders.

**10** Join the two backing pieces with a lengthwise seam. Press the seam open. Layer the quilt top with the batting and backing and baste the three layers together with quilter's curved safety pins.

**11** Change the machine foot to a walking foot. Using quilting thread, machine quilt in-the-ditch around all the blocks.

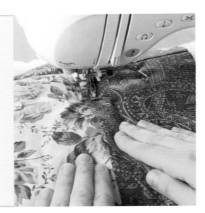

**12** Trim the excess backing and batting even with the quilt edges. Join the binding strips into one long strip with diagonal seams and press in half with wrong sides facing to make a double-fold binding. Bind the edges of the quilt, mitering the corners.

# Nine-Patch Pillowcase

## YOU WILL NEED

**For standard pillowcase 20 x 30 in. (50 x 76 cm)**

Yardage based on 44-in.- (112-cm-) wide fabric with a usable width of 42 in. (106 cm)

- o Fat eighth dark green-print fabric for blocks
- o Fat eighth light green-print fabric for blocks
- o 1¾ yd. (1.4 m) pink rose-print fabric for pillowcase and backing for pieced strip
- o 3½ x 20½ in. (9 x 51.5 cm) backing fabric for pieced strip
- o Rotary cutter, quilter's ruler, and cutting mat
- o Sewing thread

*See* Techniques book, pages 38–42, for quilting techniques; page 43 for making a double-fold binding.

## CUTTING LIST

All measurements include ¼-in. (0.75-cm) seam allowances.

**Dark green print**

○ Cut 3 strips 1½ x 22 in. (4 x 56 cm)

**Light green print**

○ Cut 3 strips 1½ in. x 22 in. (4 x 56 cm)

**Pink rose print**

○ Cut one rectangle 20½ x 37½ in. (51.5 x 95 cm) for pillowcase back.

○ Cut one rectangle 20½ x 27 in. (51.5 x 68.5 cm) for pillowcase front.

○ Cut one strip 1½ x 20½ in. (4 x 51.5 cm) for binding.

○ Cut one 3½- x 20½-in. (9- x 51.5-cm) backing for pieced strip

**1** Make a strip set from two strips of dark green print and one strip of light green print. Make another strip set from two strips of light green print and one strip of dark green print.

**2** Crosscut each strip set into ten 1½-in. (4-cm) segments until you have a total of 20 units. Stitch the units together, alternating the light and dark patch arrangement, to make a pieced border.

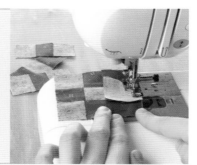

**3** Pin the pieced border along one short edge of the pillowcase front with right sides facing. Pin the rose-print backing strip right side to wrong side of pillowcase front along the same short edge. Stitch through all three layers along the short edge, then open out the border and backing strip and press.

**4** Press the binding strip in half, wrong sides facing. With right sides facing, align and pin one edge of the binding with the raw edges of the border and backing strip. Pin and stitch. Turn the binding to the back, press under ¼ in. (0.75 cm) along the long edge and slip stitch.

**5** On one short edge of the pillowcase back, turn under a ½-in. (1.5-cm) double hem and stitch. With right sides facing and raw edges aligned, pin the pillowcase back to the front, bringing excess hemmed fabric around the border end of the front to form a flap. Stitch the three sides, leaving the flap end open.

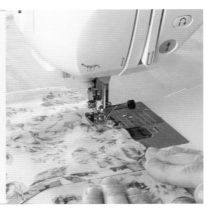

**6** Finish the raw edges of the seams with machine zigzag stitch. Turn the pillowcase right side out and press.

# Ohio Star Wall Hanging

## YOU WILL NEED

**For wall hanging 10 x 10 in. (25 x 25 cm)**

- Fat quarter pink rose print
- Fat eighth dark green print
- Fat eighth light green print
- Fat quarter dark red print
- Batting, 10 x 10 in. (25 x 25 cm)
- Cutting, quilting, and hanging equipment as for Nine-Patch Bed Quilt

Make up as for the Ohio Star wall hanging on page 7, but substitute pink rose print for blue gingham, dark green print for pink check, light green print for blue-green check, and dark red print for plain green.

## CUTTING LIST

All measurements include ¼-in. (0.75-mm) seam allowances.

**Pink rose print**

- Cut 1 strip 4¼ x 22 in. (11 x 56 cm). Cut into 5 squares 4¼ x 4¼ in. (11 x 11 cm).

**Dark green print**

- Cut 1 strip 4¼ x 9 in. (11 x 23 cm). Cut into two squares 4¼ x 4¼ in. (11 x 11 cm).

**Light green print**

- Cut 1 square 4¼ x 4¼ in. (11 x 11 cm).

**Dark red print**

- Cut square 10 x 10 in. (25.5 x 25.5 cm) for backing.
- Cut 2 strips 1½ x 9½ in. (4 x 24 cm) for binding.
- Cut 2 strips 1½ x 10 ½ in. (4 x 27 cm) for binding.

## Quilting Plus

*If you would like to quilt your hanging, add an extra 1 in. (2.5 cm) all around the backing and batting. Quilt in-the-ditch, then trim excess backing and batting even with the block edges.*

# Amish Pillow

The Amish people traditionally used rich colors and simple shapes in their patchwork designs. This pillow, with its bands of deep crimson and green set within a straightforward overlapped border, follows their example.

The vertical bands are ideal to show off a variety of easy-to-stitch machine-quilted border designs—hearts, waves, and curving lines.

Skill Level: Beginner

25

# Amish Pillow

## YOU WILL NEED

**For pillow 14 x 14 in. (36 x 36 cm)**

Yardage based on 44-in.- (112-cm-) wide fabric with a usable width of 42 in. (106 cm)

- Fat eighth maroon marbled print for panel bands
- Fat eighth green spotted print for panel bands
- Fat eighth aqua spotted print for narrow border
- ½ yd. (0.5 m) purple spotted print for wide border and cushion back
- Cotton fabric for panel backing, 16 x 16 in. (40 x 40 cm)
- Batting, 16 x 16 in. (40 x 40 cm)
- Rotary cutter, quilter's ruler, and cutting mat
- Sewing thread
- Soapstone or quilter's silver marking pencil
- Quilter's safety pins
- Machine quilting thread
- Pillow form 15 x 15 in. (38 x 38 cm)

## CUTTING LIST

All measurements include ¼-in. (7.5-mm) seam allowances.

**Maroon marbled print**

- Cut 3 strips 2½ x 10½ in. (6.5 x 26.5 cm).

**Green spotted print**

- Cut 2 strips 2½ x 10½ in. (6.5 x 26.5 cm).

**Aqua spotted print**

- Cut 2 strips 1 x 10½ in. (3 x 26.5 cm) and 2 strips 1 x 11½ in. (3 x 29.5 cm) for narrow border.

**Purple spotted print**

- Cut square 16 x 16 in. (40 x 40 cm) for cushion back.
- Cut 2 strips 2 x 11½ in. (5.5 x 29.5 cm) and 2 strips 2 x 14½ in. (5.5 x 37.5 cm) for wide border.

*Amish pillow layout*

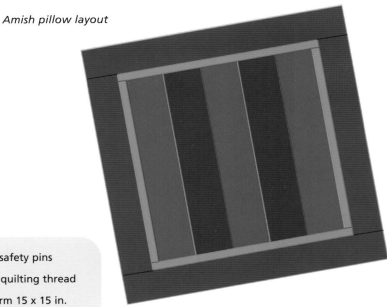

1 Following the order shown on the layout diagram opposite, pin and stitch the maroon and green strips together along their long edges to make the center panel. Press the seam allowances toward the maroon fabric.

2 Pin and stitch the two shorter aqua border strips to the sides of the panel. Press the seam allowances toward the borders. Pin and stitch the two longer aqua border strips to the top and bottom of the panel. Press the seam allowances toward the borders.

3 Pin and stitch the shorter purple border strips to the sides of the narrow border. Press the seam allowances toward the borders. Pin and stitch longer purple border strips to the top and bottom of the narrow border. Press the seam allowances toward the borders.

## Thread Color

*When you are piecing fabrics in several different colors, use a neutral-colored thread in your machine—a mid-gray or green blue would be suitable for the Amish pillow. It will blend with all the fabrics, so you won't need to keep changing your threads.*

**4** Using a permanent black marking pen, trace the appropriate quilting designs from page 92 of the Projects book onto freezer paper. Place each band of the panel over the traced design on a light box and trace the design onto the fabric with a soapstone or quilter's silver pencil.

**5** Layer the pillow top with the batting and cotton backing and baste the three layers together with quilter's safety pins.

**6** Change your machine foot to a walking foot. Using machine quilting thread, machine stitch around the marked quilting motifs. Start with the center band and work outward, then quilt around the inner and outer edges of the narrow border.

## Use a Window

*If you haven't got a light box to use when marking the quilting designs onto the fabric, you can achieve a similar effect by taping the design and fabric to a window on a bright day. The designs should show clearly through the fabric, and you can then mark the design with a quilter's pencil.*

See Techniques book, pages 38–42, for quilting techniques.

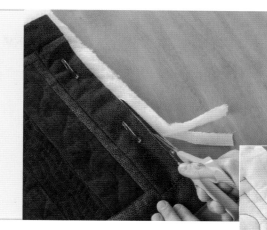

7 | Trim the excess cotton backing fabric and batting even with the edges of the pillow top. Trim the large square of purple spotted fabric for the pillow back to the same size as the pillow top. With right sides facing, pin and stitch the pillow back to the pillow top around the top and sides, leaving the bottom edge open.

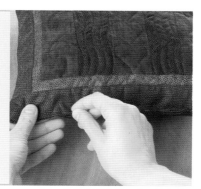

8 | Clip the corners and trim away some of the batting in the seam allowances. Turn the pillow cover right side out. Insert the pillow form, turn in the raw edges along the opening, pin, and slip stitch it closed.

## Press Gently

*Once you have turned the pillow cover right side out, press it just around the very edge to set the seams. Don't place the iron on the pillow cover itself, as this will flatten the batting and spoil the contours of the quilting.*

# Christmas Table Runner

Fabrics with seasonal motifs and a touch of glitter give a festive feel to this table runner, which would look spectacular as the centerpiece of your Christmas table setting.

You'll find the pinwheel blocks easy to assemble using quick-pieced half-square triangle units. Simply add some sashing strips and a border, and sew on a backing to complete the runner. Make the matching mantel cover on page 37 for an exciting Christmas duo.

Skill Level: Beginner

# Christmas Table Runner

## CUTTING LIST

All measurements include ¼-in.
(0.75-cm) seam allowances.

**Red metallic fabric**

- Cut 1 strip 2⅞ x 42 in.
  (7.5 x 106 cm). Cut strip into
  12 squares 2⅞ x 2⅞ in.
  (7.5 x 7.5 cm).

- Cut 2 squares 2½ x 2½ in.
  (6.5 x 6.5 cm) for corner squares.

**Cream metallic fabric**

- Cut 2 strips 2⅞ x 42 in.
  (7.5 x 106 cm). Cut strips into
  24 squares 2⅞ x 2⅞ in.
  (7.5 x 7.5 cm).

**Green swirls print**

- Cut 1 strip 2⅞ x 42 in.
  (7.5 x 106 cm). Cut strip into
  12 squares 2⅞ x 2⅞ in.
  (7.5 x 7.5 cm).

- Cut 2 squares 2½ x 2½ in.
  (6.5 x 6.5 cm) for corner squares.

**Green holly print**

- Cut 2 strips 2½ x 8½ in.
  (6.5 x 21.5 cm) for sashing.

- Cut 2 strips 2½ x 8½ in.
  (6.5 x 21.5 cm) and 2 strips
  2½ x 28½ in. (6.5 x 71.5 cm) for
  border.

- Cut piece 12½ x 32½ in.
  (31.5 x 81.5 cm) for backing.

*Table runner layout*

1  From one red metallic and one cream metallic square, make two half-square triangle units. Make a total of 24 red-and-cream half-square triangle units. Press the seam allowances toward the red triangles.

## Be Accurate!

*Make sure you mark, stitch, and cut the half-square triangle units accurately. This will ensure that the points of the pinwheel blocks meet precisely in the center when you stitch the four units together.*

2  In the same way, use one green swirl and one cream metallic square to make two half-square triangle units. Make a total of 24 green-and-cream half-square triangle units. Press the seam allowances toward the green triangles.

3  Arrange four of the red-and-cream units in a pinwheel block pattern. Stitch the units together in horizontal pairs. Press the seam allowances toward the red triangles.

*See* Techniques book, page 26, for quick-piecing half-square triangle units.

**4** Stitch together the two red-and-cream pairs, matching the seams, to form the first pinwheel block. Press the seam allowance open or to one side.

**5** Repeat steps 3 and 4 to make a total of six red-and-cream pinwheel blocks. In the same way, make a total of six green-and-cream pinwheel blocks.

**7** Stitch the two pairs together, matching the seams, to complete one center panel. Press the seam allowances open.

**6** Arrange two pinwheel blocks in each color scheme to form one of the center panels. Stitch the blocks together in horizontal pairs. Press the seam allowances to one side.

*See* Techniques book, page 28, for assembling pieced blocks.

## Nest Seams

*When you join the red and green pinwheel blocks into pairs, press the seam allowance toward the red block each time. When you come to join the pairs in step 7, the seams will nestle neatly together.*

8 Repeat steps 6 and 7 with the remaining pinwheel blocks to make two more center panels. Stitch them together with two green holly sashing strips in between. Press seam allowances toward sashing strips. Stitch a short green holly border to each end.

9 Stitch a red and a green swirl corner square to each end of the two long green holly border strips. Stitch these strips along each long side of the runner so that the matching squares are diagonally opposite each other.

10 With right sides facing, stitch the backing fabric to the runner, leaving an opening at one short end for turning. Turn the runner right side out and slip stitch the opening closed.

# Pinwheel Mantel Cover

Dress up your fireplace this Christmas with a fabulous mantel cover that coordinates with the Christmas Table Runner on page 32. It features the similar pinwheel blocks and also has tree blocks forming pennants along the lower edge.

Choose fabric with a festive theme, combining Christmas prints with metallic plains, set off by star-spangled red sashing and borders.

Skill Level: Intermediate

# Pinwheel Mantel Cover

**For mantel cover
49 x 19 in. (125 x 48 cm)**

Yardage based on 44-in.-
(112-cm-) wide fabric with
a usable width of 42 in.
(106 cm)

- Fat eighth each of green
  print and blue print

- 1¼ yd. (1.2 m) cream
  metallic fabric

- 1¾ yd. (1.6 m) red star print

- Fat quarter green metallic
  fabric

- Rotary cutter, quilter's ruler,
  and cutting mat

- Sewing thread

## CUTTING LIST

All measurements include ¼-in.
(0.75-cm) seam allowances.

**Green print**

- Cut 2 strips 2⅞ x 22 in. (7.5 x
  56 cm). Cut strips into 10 squares
  2⅞ x 2⅞ in. (7.5 x 7.5 cm).

**Cream metallic fabric**

- Cut 2 strips 2⅞ x 42 in. (7.5 x
  106 cm). Cut strips into 20 squares
  2⅞ x 2⅞ in. (7.5 x 7.5 cm).

- Cut patches for trees and pennants
  as instructed in steps 5, 6, 7, and 8.

**Blue print**

- Cut 2 strips 2⅞ x 22 in.
  (7.5 x 56 cm). Cut strips into 10
  squares 2⅞ x 2⅞ in. (7.5 x 7.5 cm).

- Cut patches for trunks as instructed
  in step 6.

**Red star print**

- Cut two pieces 6 x 25 in.
  (15.5 x 63.5 cm) for top border.

- Cut 6 strips 2 x 6 in.
  (5.5 x 15.5 cm) and 5 strips 2 x
  8½ in. (5.5 x 21.5 cm) for sashing.

- Cut 2 pieces 11 ½ x 25 in.
  (29.5 x 63.5 cm) for backing.

- Cut patches for trunks and
  pennants as instructed in
  steps 6, 7, and 8.

**Green metallic fabric**

- Cut patches for trees as instructed
  in step 5.

*Mantel cover layout*

1 | Take the ten green-print squares and ten of the cream metallic squares and make 20 half-square triangle units. Join the units together in pairs. Press. Stitch two pairs together to make a pinwheel block. Press. Make a total of five green/cream pinwheel blocks.

2 | Repeat step 1, using the ten blue-print squares and the remaining ten cream metallic squares to make five blue/cream pinwheel blocks. Press. Join a green/cream pinwheel block to a blue/cream pinwheel block. Make five pairs of pinwheel blocks.

4 | Join these sections with the six 2- x 6-in. (5- x 15- cm) vertical sashing strips. Press. Join the two top border pieces along one short edge, press, then stitch the border to the top edge of the pinwheel panel. Press.

3 | Using the five red star sashing strips that measure 2 x 8½ in. (5.5 x 21.5 cm), pin and stitch a strip to the bottom edge of each pair of blocks.

*See* Techniques book, page 26, for quick-piecing half-square triangle units.

**5** Cut the patch sizes shown at right, and make each layer of the green tree as follows. Place a cream rectangle at a right angle to a green metallic rectangle. Mark a diagonal across the corner. Stitch along the line, trim seam to ¼ in. (0.75 cm), and press toward the green. Repeat on the other side.

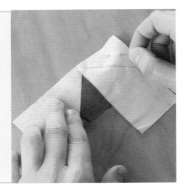

**6** To make the trunk, stitch two 2- x 2¼-in. (5- x 5.5-cm) cream rectangles to each side of a 2 x 2-in. (5- x 5-cm) red square. Center tree and trunk rows under one another and join. Repeat steps 5 and 6 to make a total of three green tree blocks. Trim block width to 5½ in. (14 cm).

**7** Cut a 3½- x 5½-in. (9- x 14-cm) cream rectangle in half diagonally to make two right-angled triangles. Stitch one triangle to each side of a tree unit. Cut an equilateral triangle with 3¾-in. (9.5-cm) sides and stitch to the center of the base. Trim the lower corners at an angle to line up with the two side triangles. Repeat for all triangular tree pennants.

**Tree, top row:** Stitch two 2- x 3½-in. (5- x 9-cm) cream metallic rectangles to a 2- x 3½-in. (5- x 9-cm) green metallic rectangle.

**Tree, middle row:** Stitch two 2- x 3-in. (5- x 7.5-cm) cream metallic rectangles to a 2- x 4-in. (5- x 10-cm) green metallic rectangle.

**Tree, bottom row:** Stitch two 2- x 2½-in. (5- x 6-cm) cream metallic rectangles to a 2- x 5-in. (5- x 12.5-cm) green metallic rectangle.

**8** Cut a large cream triangle to fit the size of a triangular tree pennant. Place it on the tree pennant with right sides facing. Stitch along the sides, leaving the top open. Trim the point and turn right side out. Repeat for the remaining green tree pennants.

**9** Repeat steps 5 through 8 to make two more tree pennants, this time using the cream metallic fabric for the tree, the blue print fabric for the trunk, and the red star fabric for the background.

**10** With right sides facing and alternating the two color schemes, pin the tree pennants along the bottom edge of the pinwheel panel, taking care to center them under each pair of blocks. They will overlap slightly.

**11** Join the two red star-print backing pieces along one short edge and press the seam allowance open. With right sides facing, place the red star backing on top of the pinwheel panel with the pennants pointing inward. Stitch around three sides, leaving one short side open. Clip the corners, turn right side out, and press. Slip stitch the opening closed.

# Table Mat and Napkin

A delightful floral print is set off by spotted and striped fabric in this fresh-looking table set. The mat is padded with a heat-proof interlining, which makes it practical as well as pretty.

The pieced center panel is set on-point to create a diamond pattern, and both mat and napkin are embellished with echo quilting to emphasize the block shapes. The mat and napkin duo is quick to assemble, so why not make a set for each member of the family?

Skill Level: Beginner

# Table Mat

## YOU WILL NEED

**For table mat 12 x 16 in. (31 x 42 cm)**

Yardage based on 44-in.-(112-cm-) wide fabric with a useable width of 42 in. (106 cm)

- o Fat quarter each of pastel stripe and pink-spotted print

- o ¾ yd. (0.7 m) rose print fabric for border strips, backing and binding

- o Curtain interlining, 11½ x 15½ in. (29.5 x 40.5 cm)

- o Rotary cutter, quilter's ruler, and cutting mat

- o Sewing thread

- o Water-soluble marking pen

- o Quilter's safety pins

- o Pink thread for machine quilting

## CUTTING LIST

All measurements include ¼-in. (0.75-cm) seam allowances.

**Pastel stripe**

- o Cut 1 strip 4⅜ x 22 in. (11.5 x 56 cm). Cut strip into 4 squares 4⅜ x 4⅜ in. (11.5 x 11.5 cm). Cut another strip if you want to cut squares with an identical stripe pattern for matching the half-square triangles.

**Pink spotted print**

- o Cut 1 strip 3⅜ x 6¾ in. (9 x 18 cm).

Cut strip into 2 squares 3⅜ x 3⅜ in. (9 x 9 cm) for corner triangles.

- o Cut 1 square 6¼ x 6¼ in. (16.5 x 16.5 cm) for setting triangles.

**Rose print**

- o Cut 2 strips 3½ x 15½ in. (9 x 40.5 cm) for border.

- o Cut 1 piece 11½ x 15½ in. (29.5 x 40.5 cm) for backing.

- o Cut 3 strips 1½ x 27 in. (4 x 69 cm) for binding.

*Table mat layout*

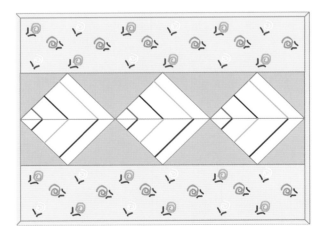

1 Using two different squares of the pastel stripe fabric, make two half-square triangle units for the central panel of the mat, matching the stripes if you wish. Repeat to make a third half-square triangle unit.

## Extra Mats

*If you are making several table mats, you can keep the fourth striped half-square triangle unit left over from step 1 to use for an additional mat.*

2 From the large square of pink-spotted fabric, cut four quarter-square triangles to make setting triangles for the central panel. From the two small squares of pink-spotted fabric, cut four half-square triangles to make corner triangles for the panel.

3 Following the table mat layout opposite, lay out the units. To join them into diagonal sections, begin by joining the bottom left-hand corner triangle, the left-hand pastel stripe unit, and the top left setting triangle to make the first section.

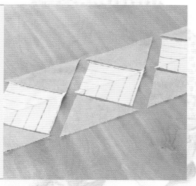

*See* Techniques book, page 26, for quick-piecing half-square and quarter-square triangle units; page 33 for setting blocks.

**4** Next, join the bottom left setting triangle, the center pastel stripe unit, and the top right setting triangle to make the center section.

## Check Twice, Sew Once

*Double-check the layout on page 44 to make sure that you are joining the correct patches at each stage of assembling the diagonal rows of the center panel. Make sure, too, that you have placed the striped squares so that the "chevron" pattern matches along the band.*

**5** Finally, join the bottom right setting triangle, the right-hand pastel stripe unit, and the top right corner triangle to make the last section.

**6** Join the three sections together as shown. Add a corner triangle at top left and bottom right. This completes the center panel.

*See Techniques book, page 33, for setting blocks.*

**7** Stitch a pink rose-print border strip to the top and bottom of the panel. Using a water-soluble marking pen, mark three rows of echo quilting at 1-in. (2.5-cm) intervals on either side of the diamond shapes in the center panel.

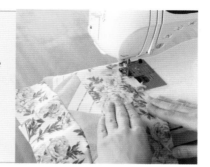

## Perfect Pads

*The curtain interlining used to pad the table mat gives it body without too much bulk and has the advantage of being heat-proof.*

**8** With the pieced table mat right side up, layer it with the curtain interlining and then the pink rose backing (wrong side up), and baste the three layers together with quilter's safety pins. With pink quilting thread in your machine, quilt along the marked lines.

**9** Square up the table mat if necessary. Join the binding strips with diagonal seams into one long strip to make a single-fold binding. Bind the edges of the mat, taking a ½-in. (1.25-cm) seam allowance on the table mat and mitering the corners.

*See* Techniques book, pages 38–42, for quilting techniques; page 45 for making a single binding.

# Napkin

## YOU WILL NEED

**For one napkin 12 x 12 in. (30 x 30 cm)**

- Fat eighth of rose print
- Fat quarter each of pink-spotted print and pastel stripe
- Fat quarter backing fabric
- Rotary cutter, quilter's ruler, and cutting mat
- Sewing thread
- Water-soluble marking pen
- Pink machine-quilting thread

*Napkin layout*

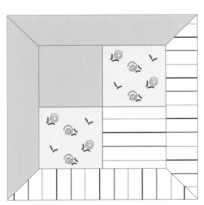

## CUTTING LIST

All measurements include ¼-in. (0.75-cm) seam allowances.

**Rose print**

- Cut 1 strip 4⅞ x 10 in. (12.5 x 25 cm). Cut into 2 squares 4⅞ x 4⅞ in. (12.5 x 12.5 cm).

**Pink-spotted print**

- Cut 2 strips 2½ x 15 in. (6.5 x 38 cm) for border.

- Cut 1 square 4½ x 4½ in. (11.5 x 11.5 cm).

**Pastel stripe**

- Cut 2 strips 2½ x 15 in. (6.5 x 38 cm) for border.

- Cut 1 square 4½ x 4½ in. (11.5 x 11.5 cm).

**1** From the two rose-print squares, make two half-square triangle units.

**2** Join the pink-spotted square to one of the rose-print half-square units for the top row of the block. Press. Join the other rose print unit to the pastel stripe square for the bottom row. Press. Join the top row to the bottom row, matching seams. Press.

*See* Techniques book, page 26, for quick-piecing half-square triangle units.

**3** Stitch the two pink-spotted border strips to the two adjacent sides of the block around the pink-spotted square, mitering the corner. Press the corner seam allowance open. Stitch the two pastel stripe border strips to the other two adjacent sides, mitering the remaining corners. Press.

**4** Cut a square of backing fabric 12½ x 12½ in. (31.5 x 31.5 cm) and pin to the pieced napkin, right sides facing. Stitch around the edge, leaving a gap for turning. Turn right side out and close the gap with slip stitching. Using a water-soluble marking pen, mark rows of echo quilting as shown on the napkin layout opposite. With pink quilting thread in your machine, quilt along marked lines.

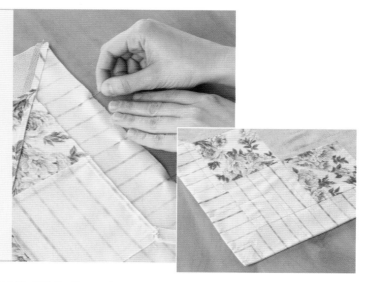

*See* Techniques book, pages 36–37, for borders with mitered corners; pages 38-42 for quilting techniques.

# Crosses Crib Set

Square patches are pieced into a diagonal cross design on this charming nursery set. The quilt and easy-to-make fitted sheet make a coordinated crib set, and the wall hanging and ruffled pillow are perfect matching accessories.

The pretty pastel solids and prints are soft cotton flannel to keep your baby warm and cozy.

Skill Level: Beginner

51

# Crib Quilt

**For crib quilt 40 x 51 in. (99 x 127 cm)**

Yardage based on 44-in.- (112-cm-) wide cotton flannel with a useable width of 42 in. (106 cm).

- 1 yd. (0.9 m) cherry print
- ½ yd. (0.5 m) each of green and pink fabric
- ¼ yd. (0.25 m) blue fabric
- 3½ yd. (3.3 m) animal print for border, binding, and backing
- Batting, 45 x 60 in. (114 x 152 cm)
- Rotary cutter, quilter's ruler, and cutting mat
- Sewing thread
- White quilter's pencil
- Quilter's safety pins
- Cotton thread for machine quilting

## CUTTING LIST

All measurements include ¼-in. (0.75-cm) seam allowances.

### Cherry print

- Cut 3 strips 4½ x 42 in. (11.5 x 106 cm). Cut strips into 23 squares 4½ x 4½ in. (11.5 x 11.5 cm).
- Cut 1 strip 6⅞ x 42 in. (17.5 x 106 cm). Cut strip into 6 squares 6⅞ x 6⅞ in. (17.5 x 17.5 cm), then cut squares twice diagonally into 24 setting triangles.
- Cut 1 strip 3¾ x 7½ in. (9.5 x 19 cm). Cut strip into 2 squares 3¾ x 3¾ in. (9.5 x 9.5 cm), then cut squares once diagonally into 4 corner triangles.

### Green fabric

- Cut 3 strips 4½ x 42 in. (11.5 x 106 cm). Cut strips into 24 squares 4½ x 4½ in. (11.5 x 11.5 cm).

### Blue fabric

- Cut 1 strip 4½ x 42 in. (11.5 x 106 cm). Cut strip into 6 squares 4½ x 4½ in. (11.5 x 11.5 cm).

### Pink fabric

- Cut 3 strips 4½ x 42 in. (11.5 x 106 cm). Cut strips into 24 squares 4½ x 4½ in. (11.5 x 11.5 cm).

### Animal print

- Cut 1 strip 4½ x 27 in. (11.5 x 69 cm). Cut strip into 6 squares 4½ x 4½ in. (11.5 x 11.5 cm) for front.
- Cut 2 lengthwise strips 3½ in. (9 cm) x length of quilt, and 2 lengthwise strips 3½ in. (9 cm) x width of quilt plus two border widths for border.
- Cut piece 42 x 53 in. (106 x 135 cm) for backing.
- Cut 4 lengthwise strips 3 x 54 in. (7.5 x 137 cm) for binding.

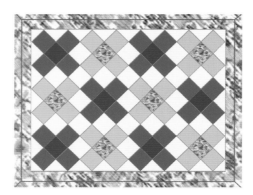

*Crib quilt layout*

**1** Following the crib quilt layout opposite, lay out the squares in the correct order on a large work surface. Starting in the top left-hand corner, make the first diagonal row by joining one cherry-print setting triangle, one green square, and another cherry-print setting triangle. Press.

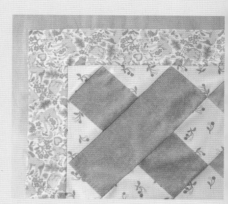

**2** Make second diagonal row by joining one cherry-print setting triangle, one green square, one blue square, another green square, and another cherry-print setting triangle. Press. Continue joining patches in diagonal rows down to the bottom right-hand corner. The rows get longer toward the quilt center, then shorter.

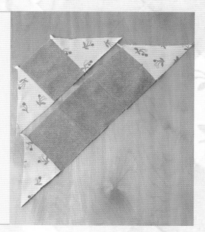

**4** Square up the quilt edges. Measure the length of the quilt through the center and cut two 3½-in.- (9-cm-) wide border strips from the animal print to fit. Stitch them to the sides of the quilt. Press the seam allowance toward the borders. Measure the width of the quilt through the center, including the width of the two border strips. Cut two more animal-print border strips to fit, and stitch them to top and bottom of the quilt. Press.

**3** Now join the diagonal rows of patches to each other in the correct order, matching seams. Add a cherry-print corner triangle at each corner to complete the quilt center.

*See* Techniques book, page 35, for making borders.

**5** Using a white quilter's pencil and ruler, mark small crosses—2 in. (5 cm) lines in each direction—in the center of the squares as guidelines for the diagonal grid.

**6** Layer the quilt top with the batting and backing. Baste the layers together with quilter's safety pins. Following the marked guidelines, machine-quilt a 4- x 4-in. (10- x 10-cm) diagonal grid across the quilt.

**7** Trim the excess batting and backing even with the quilt edges. Join the binding strips with diagonal seams into one long strip and press in half with wrong sides facing to make a double-fold binding. Bind the edges of the quilt, mitering the corners.

# Wall Hanging

## YOU WILL NEED

**For wall hanging 23 x 23 in. (56 x 56 cm)**

Yardage based on 44-in.-(112-cm-) wide cotton flannel with a usable width of 42 in. (106 cm).

o ½ yd. (0.5 m) cherry print

o ¼ yd. (0.25 m) each of green and pink fabric

o Fat eighth blue fabric

o 1¼ yd. (1.2 m) animal print

o Batting, 29 x 29 in. (75 x 75 cm)

o Rotary cutter, quilter's ruler, and cutting mat

o Sewing thread

o Quilter's safety pins

o Cotton thread for machine quilting

o 27-in. (69-cm) length of doweling

**See photo for layout design**

*See* Techniques book, pages 38–42, for quilting techniques; page 43 for making a double-fold binding.

## CUTTING LIST

All measurements include ¼-in. (0.75-cm) seam allowances.

### Cherry print

o Cut 1 strip 4½ x 42 in. (11.5 x 106 cm). Cut strip into 5 squares 4½ x 4½ in. (11.5 x 11.5 cm).

o Cut 1 strip 6⅞ x 22 in. (17.5 x 56 cm). Cut strip into 3 squares 6⅞ x 6⅞ in. (17.5 x 17.5 cm), then cut squares twice diagonally into 12 setting triangles.

o Cut 1 strip 3¾ x 7½ in. (9.5 x 19 cm). Cut strip into 2 squares 3¾ x 3¾ in. (9.5 x 9.5 cm). Cut squares once diagonally into 4 corner triangles.

### Green fabric

o Cut 1 strip 4½ x 42 in. (11.5 x 106 cm). Cut strip into 8 squares 4½ x 4½ in. (11.5 x 11.5 cm).

### Pink fabric

o Cut 1 strip 4½ x 42 in. (11.5 x 106 cm). Cut strip into 8 squares 4½ x 4½ in. (11.5 x 11.5 cm).

### Blue fabric

o Cut 1 strip 4½ x 9 in. (11.5 x 23 cm). Cut strip into 2 squares 4½ x 4½ in. (11.5 x 11.5 cm).

### Animal print

o For squares, cut 1 strip 4½ x 9 in. (11.5 x 23 cm). Cut strip into 2 squares 4½ x 4½ in. (11.5 x 11.5 cm).

o For backing, cut a square 29 x 29 in. (75 x 75 cm).

o For binding, cut 3 lengthwise strips 1½ x 45 in. (4 x 115 cm).

o For tabs, cut 2 pieces 6½ x 8½ in. (16.5 x 21.5 cm).

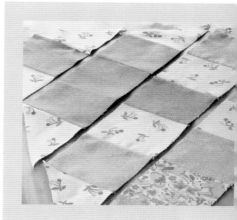

2 Make the second diagonal row by joining one cherry-print setting triangle, one green square, one blue square, another green square, and another cherry-print setting triangle. Press. Continue joining the patches in diagonal rows following the wall-hanging layout until you complete them all.

1 Following the layout of the wall-hanging photo on page 50, lay out the squares. Starting in top left-hand corner, make first diagonal row by joining one cherry-print setting triangle, one green square, and another cherry-print setting triangle.

3 | Now join the diagonal rows of patches to each other. Add a cherry-print corner triangle at the two opposite corners to complete the design. Square up the wall hanging if necessary.

4 | Mark guidelines for quilting as for Crib Quilt, page 54, step 5. Layer the pieced wall hanging with batting and backing, and baste the three layers together with quilter's safety pins. Machine-quilt a 4- x 4-in. (10- x 10-cm) diagonal grid across the wall hanging.

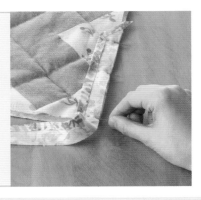

5 | Trim excess batting and backing even with the edges of the quilt sandwich. Join the binding strips with diagonal seams into one strip to make a single-fold binding. Pin and stitch binding to quilt edges with a ½ in. (1 cm) seam allowance. Miter the corners.

6 | Fold the tab pieces in half lengthwise with right sides facing and stitch along the long edges. Turn them right side out. Tuck in the raw edges, fold the tabs in half, and slip stitch them just below the top and 2¾ in. (7cm) in from the sides of the wall hanging. Hang it from a length of doweling.

See Techniques book, pages 38–42, for quilting techniques; page 45 for making a single binding.

# Pillow

## YOU WILL NEED

**11¼ x 11¼ in. (28 x 28 cm) for pillow with 3-in. (7.5-cm) ruffle**

Yardage based on 44-in.-(112-cm-) wide cotton flannel with a usable width of 42 in. (106 cm).

- Fat quarter cherry print
- Fat eighth each of green and blue fabric
- 1¼ yd. (1.2 m) animal print
- ¾ yd. (0.7 m) backing fabric
- Batting, 16 x 16 in. (40 x 40 cm)
- Sewing thread
- Quilting thread for crib quilt, page 52
- Pillow form, 11 x 11 in. (28 x 28 cm)

## CUTTING LIST

All measurements include ¼-in. (0.75-cm) seam allowances.

### Cherry print

- Cut 1 square 6⅞ x 6⅞ in. (17.5 x 17.5 cm), then cut square twice diagonally into 4 setting triangles.
- Cut 1 strip 3¾ x 7½ in. (9.5 x 19 cm). Cut strip into 2 squares 3¾ x 3¾ in. (9.5 x 9.5 cm), then cut squares once diagonally into 4 corner triangles.

### Green fabric

- Cut 1 strip 4½ x 22 in. (11.5 x 56 cm). Cut strip into 4 squares 4½ x 4½ in. (11.5 x 11.5 cm).

### Blue fabric

- Cut 1 square 4½ x 4½ in. (11.5 x 11.5 cm).

### Backing fabric

- Cut a 16 x 16 in. (40 x 40 cm) square.

### Animal print

- For double ruffle, cut 3 strips 6½ x 31 in. (16.5 x 79 cm).
- For backing, cut piece 16 x 16 in. (40 x 40 cm).
- For border, cut 4 strips 1 x 14 in. (3 x 36 cm).

1 Join the patches in three diagonal rows (see crib quilt, page 53, steps 1 and 2). Now join the diagonal rows of patches to each other in the correct order. Add a cherry-print corner triangle at each corner.

**2** Stitch a narrow border strip to two opposite sides of the block. Trim even with the top and bottom. Stitch a narrow border strip to the top and bottom of the block. Trim to fit.

**3** Mark guidelines for quilting as for Crib Quilt, page 54, step 5. Layer the pillow top with batting and backing, and baste the layers together with quilter's safety pins. Machine-quilt a 4- x 4-in. (10- x 10-cm) diagonal grid across the quilt. Trim excess batting and backing even with the edges of the quilt sandwich.

**5** With right sides facing, pin pillow backing to the pillow front with ruffle sandwiched between. Stitch around three sides, leaving the bottom edge open. Turn right side out. Insert pillow form. Slip stitch the opening closed.

**4** With right sides facing, join the strips for the ruffle along the short edges to form a circle. Fold in half with wrong sides facing, and work two rows of machine-gathering stitches along the raw edges. Pin the ruffle evenly around the block with right sides facing and raw edges aligned. Baste and stitch. Remove gathering threads.

## Perfect Ruffles

*For an even ruffle, mark the circle of fabric into four equal sections with pins. When attaching the ruffle, position the pins at the center of each side. Gather fabric evenly between the pins.*

# Crib Sheet

## YOU WILL NEED

**For one fitted sheet to fit any crib mattress—(mattress shown measures 28 x 52 x 5 in. (71 x 132 x 12.5 cm))**

o 2 yd. (1.9 m) animal-print cotton flannel

## CUTTING LIST

All measurements include ¼-in. (0.75-cm) seam allowances.

**Animal print**

o Measure the length, width, and depth of the crib mattress. Cut a rectangle of fabric that is two times the depth plus the width across the top and bottom edges, and two times the depth plus the length along the side edges.

o Cut a square the size of the mattress depth out of each of the four corners of the rectangle. Save these squares.

1 At one corner of the animal-print rectangle, place the two adjacent cut edges together with right sides facing, pin, and stitch. Repeat at the remaining three corners.

2 To make corner triangles, press the four small cutout squares in half diagonally, wrong sides facing. With right sides facing and raw edges aligned, pin and stitch one triangle into a corner of the animal-print rectangle. Repeat at remaining three corners.

3 Finish the raw edges of the sheet with machine zigzag stitch. Turn under a ¼-in. (0.75-cm) hem between the corner triangles and stitch. Turn the sheet right side out.

# Flying Geese Backpack

Carry your possessions with style in this colorful musical backpack. Its striking red-and-white flying geese borders and melodious print give it a harmonious blend of spirit and whimsy.

Lined and lightly padded, the backpack is quilted in-the-ditch around the borders and has straight grid quilting across the main fabric. Inside is a useful pocket to keep your cell phone handy.

## Skill Level: Advanced

# Flying Geese Backpack

## YOU WILL NEED

**For backpack 15 in. (38 cm) high, 12 in. (30 cm) across, 5 ½ in. (14 cm) deep**

Yardage based on 44-in.- (112-cm-) wide fabric with a usable width of 42 in. (106 cm).
Allow extra yardage if you wish to center motifs.

- ½ yd. (0.5 m) each of instruments print and white notes print
- ¼ yd. (0.25 m) red notes print
- 1½ yd. (1.4 m) orchestra print
- Batting, 35 x 35 in. (90 x 90 cm)
- Rotary cutter, quilter's ruler, and cutting mat
- Sewing thread
- Quilter's safety pins
- Gray thread for machine quilting

- 1 yd. (0.9 m) lightweight sew-in interfacing for pocket and straps
- Bodkin needle
- 2⅜ yd. (2.1m) cord for drawstring
- Hook-and-loop tape for closing flap

## CUTTING LIST

All measurements include ¼-in. (0.75-cm) seam allowances, unless stated otherwise.

**White notes print**

- Cut 2 strips 2⅜ x 42 in. (6.5 x 106 cm). Cut strips into 23 squares 2⅜ x 2⅜ in. (6.5 x 6.5 cm).
- Cut 1 piece 5½ x 7 in. (14 x 18 cm) for cell phone pocket.

**Red notes print**

- Cut 1 strip 4¼ x 42 in. (11 x 106 cm). Cut strip into 6 squares 4¼ x 4¼ in. (11 x 11 cm).

**Instruments print**

- Cut 2 strips 2 x 16¼ in. (5.5 x 43 cm) for top backpack border; cut 2 strips 2⅜ x 16¼ in. (6.25 x 43 cm) for bottom backpack border.

- Cut 2 strips 2 x 13¼ in. (5.5 x 35 cm); 1 strip 2 x 9½ in. (5.5 x 25 cm); and 1 strip 2 x 5 in. (5.5 x 13.5 cm) for flap borders.

**Orchestra print**

- Cut 2 pieces 11¼ x 16¼ in. (28.5 x 43 cm) for front and back.
- Cut 2 pieces 16¼ x 17¼ in. (43 x 44 cm) for front and back lining.
- Cut 2 pieces 6¾ x 12¾ in. (17 x 32.5 cm) for front and back lining.
- Cut 1 piece 5 x 6½ in. (13.5 x 16.5 cm) for flap; cut 1 piece 8 x 12½ in. (21.5 x 32 cm) for flap lining.
- Cut 2 strips 3½ x 28 in. (9 x 71 cm) for straps.
- Cut 1 strip 3½ x 8¼ in. (9 x 21 cm) for carrying handle.

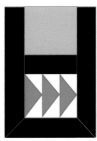

*Backpack layout*

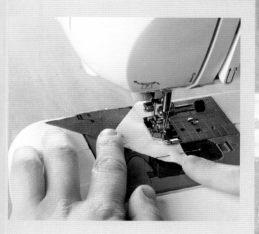

**1** From the 2⅜- x 2⅜-in. (6.5- x 6.5-cm) white note squares, cut 52 half-square triangles. From the 4¼- x 4¼-in. (11- x 11-cm) red note squares, cut 23 quarter-square triangles. To assemble one flying geese unit, stitch a white background triangle to the right-hand side of a red-notes print goose triangle, aligning the bottom edges. Press the seam allowance toward the red triangle.

**2** Complete the flying geese unit by stitching a second white background triangle to the left-hand side of the red goose triangle, aligning the bottom edges. Repeat steps 1 and 2 to make a total of 23 geese units.

**3** Referring to the backpack layout, and making sure the "geese" are all pointing the same way, stitch ten units together to make each long panel for the front and back of the backpack. Stitch three geese units together to make the short panel for the flap.

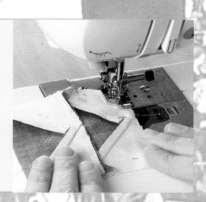

**4** With right sides facing and matching center points, stitch the 2-in. (5.5-cm) border along top edges of the long geese panels and the 2⅜-in. (6.25-cm) border along bottom edges. Stitch the shortest border to the top edge of the short geese panel. Press seam allowances toward the borders.

**5** Right sides facing, align the top edges of the long borders with the long bottom edge of front and back. Pin and stitch. Stitch top edge of the short flap border to one short edge of the orchestra print flap. Press all seam allowances toward the borders.

**6** Stitch two long borders to flap sides and shorter border to flap base, mitering corners. Press. Pin batting to wrong side of flap with quilter's safety pins. With right sides facing, stitch lining to flap along sides and base. Clip corners. Turn right side out. Press.

**7** Layer the front and back with the batting and lining. Baste the layers together with quilter's safety pins. Quilt a 2-in. (5-cm) straight grid across the front, back, and flap. Machine-quilt in-the-ditch around all the borders. Machine-baste across lower edges.

**8** Layer the base with batting and lining, and machine-quilt a 2-in. (5-cm) straight grid as in step 7. Round off each corner by cutting a simple curved template. On scrap paper, draw a quarter circle with a 2⅜-in. (6-cm) radius. Cut out, pin to the base with the curved edge at the corner, and cut off excess fabric around the curve.

*See* Techniques book, pages 36–37, for borders with mitered corners; pages 38–42 for quilting techniques.

**10** Pin interfacing to wrong side of straps and handle. Fold in half lengthwise, right sides facing. Stitch the long edges. Turn right side out with a bodkin. Press. Baste ends of the handle ¾ in. (2 cm) and straps 1½ in. (4 cm) inside side edges on right side of flap.

**9** Cut interfacing to match pocket and pin together. Press under ½ in. (1.3 cm), then ¾ in. (2 cm) at top edge. Stitch close to inner pressed edge. Make two pleats in lower edge to make width 3¾ in. (9.5 cm) and baste. Press under ⅝ in. (1.5 cm) on raw edges. Pin pocket to center of wrong side of back 5½ in. (14 cm) below upper edge. Stitch side and lower edges, reinforcing the stitching at each end of the seam.

**11** Pin and stitch the flap to the center of the back, right sides facing, 4¾ in. (12 cm) below upper edge. Press flap to right side. Stitch close to seam, then ¼ in. (0.5 cm) below. Baste strap ends to lower edge 4¾ in. (12 cm) inside side edges. Finish side and upper edges with zigzag stitching. Right sides facing and taking ⅝-in. (1.5-cm) seam allowance, stitch side seams, leaving a ¾-in. (2-cm) gap 1¾ in. (4.5 cm) below top edge. Press seam allowances open.

**12** Press upper edge to inside for 1⅝ in. (4 cm). Stitch close to pressed edge, then 1 in. (2.5 cm) below to form channel. Cut cord in half and thread through channel using the bodkin, having each cord emerge through its same hole. Knot ends together. Stitch the base to the lower edge, right sides facing, taking ⅝-in. (1.5-cm) seam allowance. Finish raw edges with zigzag stitch and turn through to right-side. Stitch on hook-and-loop tape to fasten flap.

# Shower Curtain

This spectacular shower curtain will be the focal point of your bathroom décor. Crazy patchwork blocks, pieced from randomly cut fabric patches, are alternated with print blocks.
The blue-and-green theme creates a fresh-looking color scheme that will complement any bathroom.

The curtain is fully lined with a coordinating backing fabric. Hang an ordinary waterproof shower curtain behind it to keep it from getting wet.

Skill Level: Intermediate

# Shower Curtain

## YOU WILL NEED

**For shower curtain 72 x 72 in. (184 x 184 cm).**

Yardage based on 44-in.- (112-cm-) wide fabric with a usable width of 42 in. (106 cm)

o 1¼ yd. (1.2 m) each of blue/green water print and blue/green trees print for plain blocks

o ½ yd. (0.5 m) each of five assorted blue-and-green-print fabrics for crazy blocks

o 2¼ yd. (2.1 m) of blue/yellow leaf print for wide border

o 4½ yd. (4.2 m) of dark blue print for narrow border and backing

o 3 yd. (2.7 m) of nonwoven interfacing, 36 in. (90 cm) wide, for foundation

o 1 yd. (1 m) of iron-on interfacing

o Rotary cutter, quilter's ruler, and cutting mat

o Sewing thread

o Machine embroidery thread

o Eyelet kit

o Hanging hooks

## CUTTING LIST

All measurements include ¼-in. (0.75-cm) seam allowances.

**Blue/green water print**

o Cut 3 strips 9½ x 42 in. (24.5 x 106 cm). Cut strips into 12 squares 9½ x 9½ in. (24.5 x 24.5 cm).

**Blue/green trees print**

o Cut 3 strips 9½ x 42 in. (24.5 x 106 cm). Cut strips into 12 squares 9½ x 9½ in. (24.5 x 24.5 cm).

**Foundation fabric**

o Cut 9 strips 10 x 36 in. (25.5 x 90 cm). Cut strips into 25 squares 10 x 10 in. (25.5 x 25.5 cm).

**Dark blue print**

o Cut 2 lengthwise strips 1½ in. (4 cm) x length of quilt, and 2 lengthwise strips 1½ in. (4 cm) x width of quilt center plus 2 border widths for narrow border.

**Blue/yellow leaf print**

o Cut 2 pieces 78 x 39 in. (198 x 100 cm) for backing.

o Cut 2 lengthwise strips 4 in. (10.5 cm) x length of quilt, and 2 lengthwise strips 4 in. (10.5 cm) x width of quilt plus 2 border widths for wide border.

*Shower curtain layout*

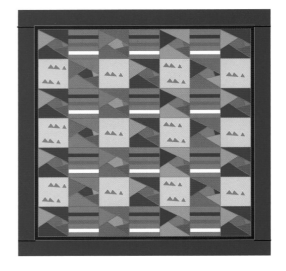

1 To make your first crazy patchwork block, use one of the foundation squares and five assorted blue-and-green fabric scraps. Cut the first randomly shaped patch and pin it to the center of the foundation.

2 Choose another fabric and cut out a second randomly shaped patch. Align it along one side of the first patch, right sides facing, and pin. Stitch it to the first patch, then flip it over to the right side and press. Trim it to line up with edges of the first patch.

4 Embellish the crazy patchwork by working machine zigzag stitch or other machine embroidery stitches along all seams between the patches.

3 Continue adding patches in the same way until you fill the foundation square. Repeat steps 1, 2, and 3 to make a total of 25 crazy patchwork blocks. Trim the blocks to measure 9½ x 9½ in. (24.5 x 24.5 cm).

  See Techniques book, page 31, for piecing crazy patchwork.

**6** Following the quilt diagram on page 68, join three crazy patchwork blocks, alternating with four blue/green trees print blocks to make the second horizontal row of the quilt. Make a total of three matching horizontal rows.

**5** Following the quilt diagram on page 68, join four of the crazy patchwork blocks, alternating with three blue/green water-print blocks to make the top horizontal row of the quilt center. Make a total of four matching horizontal rows.

**7** Join the top row of blocks to the second row of blocks, matching the seams. Press. Continue joining the horizontal rows of blocks, alternating the positions of the plain blocks as shown in the quilt layout on page 68.

**8** Measure the length of the pieced shower curtain through the center, and cut two narrow dark blue print border strips to fit. Stitch them to the sides of the shower curtain and press the seam allowances toward the border.

*See* Techniques book, page 33, for setting blocks; page 35 for making overlapped borders.

9 Measure the width of the shower curtain through the center, and cut two more narrow dark blue print border strips to fit. Stitch them to the top and bottom of the shower curtain to complete the narrow overlapped border. Press the seam allowances toward the border.

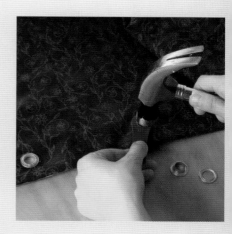

10 Cut two 4-in.- (10.5-cm-) wide strips of iron-on interfacing to fit each of the top blue/yellow leaf border strips. Iron in position. Repeat steps 8 and 9 to attach the blue/yellow borders.

12 Following the manufacturer's instructions, punch a row of eyelets along the top edge of the shower curtain to take the hanging hooks.

11 Join two dark blue print backing pieces along one long edge, right sides facing. Press this seam allowance open. Place the backing on the front of the shower curtain, right sides facing, and trim to fit. Stitch, leaving a gap along the bottom edge for turning right side out. Slip stitch the opening closed.

### Setting Spaces

*Space the eyelets at the same intervals as those in the waterproof backing curtain. Then pass the hanging hooks through pairs of eyelets along both curtains.*

# Crazy Patchwork Teddy Bear

This teddy bear is a charming character that will be loved by children and adults alike. He stands approximately 18 in. (45 cm) high and has jointed arms and legs, a felt nose, and button eyes.

Soft cotton flannel makes him a cuddly companion. Stitch him for a favorite child or just for yourself!

Skill Level: Intermediate

# Patchwork Teddy Bear

## YOU WILL NEED

For teddy bear 18 in. (45 cm) tall

Yardage based on 44-in.- (112-cm-) wide brushed cotton fabric with a usable width of 42 in. (106 cm).

- ¼ yd. (0.25 m) each of four cotton flannel fabrics in pink, cream, green, and blue
- 1 yd. (0.9 m) thin calico, 36 in. (90 cm) wide, for foundation
- Rotary cutter, quilter's ruler, and cutting mat
- Sewing thread
- Polyester fiberfill
- 2 small dark blue buttons
- Piece of dark blue felt
- Extra-strong sewing thread
- Extra-long doll needle
- 4 small mother-of-pearl buttons
- 20 in. (50 cm) of ½-in.- (1.5-cm-) wide satin ribbon

All measurements include ¼-in. (0.75-cm) seam allowances.

**Foundation fabric**

- 2 fronts as a pair
- 2 backs as a pair
- 4 arms as two pairs
- 4 legs as two pairs
- 2 heads as one pair
- 1 top of head

**Blue cotton flannel**

- 1 sole and 1 ear

**Green cotton flannel**

- 1 sole and 1 ear

**Pink cotton flannel**

- 1 ear

**Cream cotton flannel**

- 1 ear

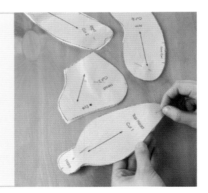

1 Enlarge the pattern pieces shown on pages 78–79 to 150% on a photocopier and cut them out. Pin them to the foundation fabric and cut them out, following the cutting list above. Fold the fabric double where a pair is required.

2 Take one of the body front pieces and the four assorted fabrics. Cut the first randomly shaped patch from one of the fabrics and pin it at the center of the foundation.

3 Choose another fabric and cut out a second randomly shaped patch. Align it along one side of the first patch with right sides facing. Pin and stitch it to the first patch, then flip it over and press. Trim it to line up with edges of first patch and edge of body.

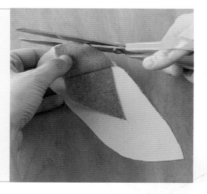

4 Continue adding patches as in step 3 to fill the body shape foundation. Give it a final press. Repeat steps 2 through 4 to cover the remaining teddy bear foundation pieces with crazy patchwork.

*See* Techniques book, page 31, for piecing crazy patchwork.

**5** Join the center seams of the front and back body pieces, leaving a small opening in the center back seam. Join the front and back body pieces together around the outer edges. Turn right side out. Stuff with fiberfill. Slip stitch the opening closed.

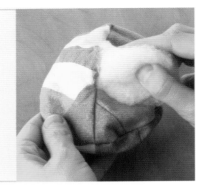

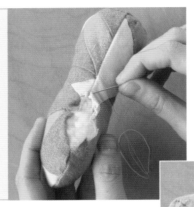

**6** Sew the arms into pairs, leaving a small opening in the back seam. Turn right side out and stuff. Sew the legs into pairs in the same way, leaving an opening in the back seam. Sew one plain sole piece into the base of each foot. Turn right side out and stuff.

## Firm Shapes

*Stuff the teddy bear firmly to create a pleasing shape. Insert small pieces of fiberfill at a time and use an unsharpened pencil to help push the stuffing well into the ends of the arms, legs, and nose.*

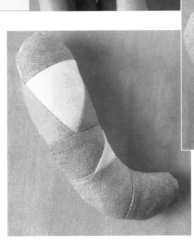

7 Make the head from the two sides and top piece. Stuff firmly. Sew on two dark blue buttons for eyes. Make two ears and sew to each side of head. Cut a small triangle of dark blue felt and slip stitch to head for the nose.

8 Using extra-strong sewing thread, sew the head to the top of the stuffed body, turning under the raw edges as you go.

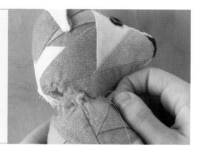

## Be Baby-Safe

*If you are making the teddy for a young child, you may prefer to substitute embroidered eyes for button eyes. To do this, work simple circles of machine satin stitch before adding the stuffing.*

9 Using extra-strong sewing thread, sew the arms and legs to the sides of the body by passing an extra-long needle back and forth through the body and the holes in the mother-of-pearl buttons several times. Pull the thread up tight and fasten off. Tie the ribbon around the neck.

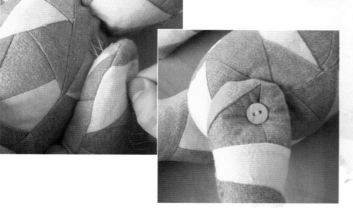

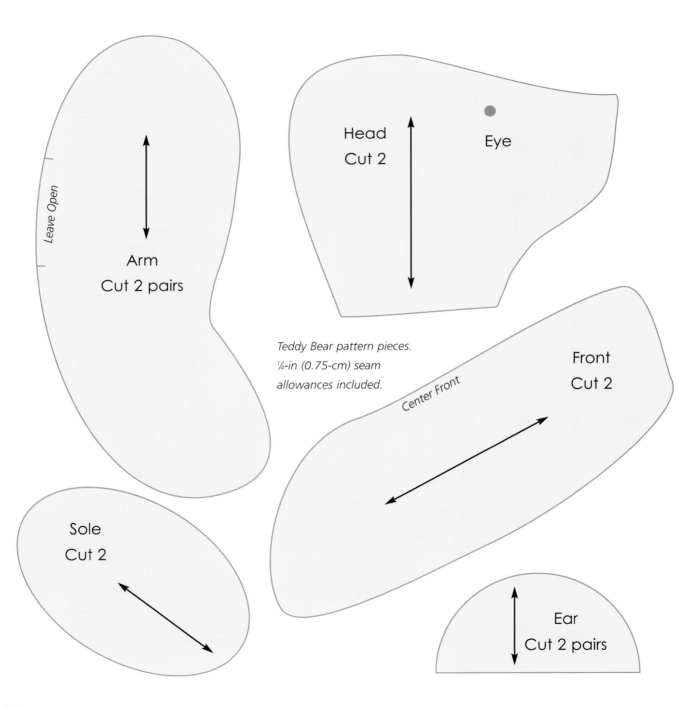

Leave Open

Arm
Cut 2 pairs

Head
Cut 2

Eye

*Teddy Bear pattern pieces.
¼-in (0.75-cm) seam
allowances included.*

Center Front

Front
Cut 2

Sole
Cut 2

Ear
Cut 2 pairs

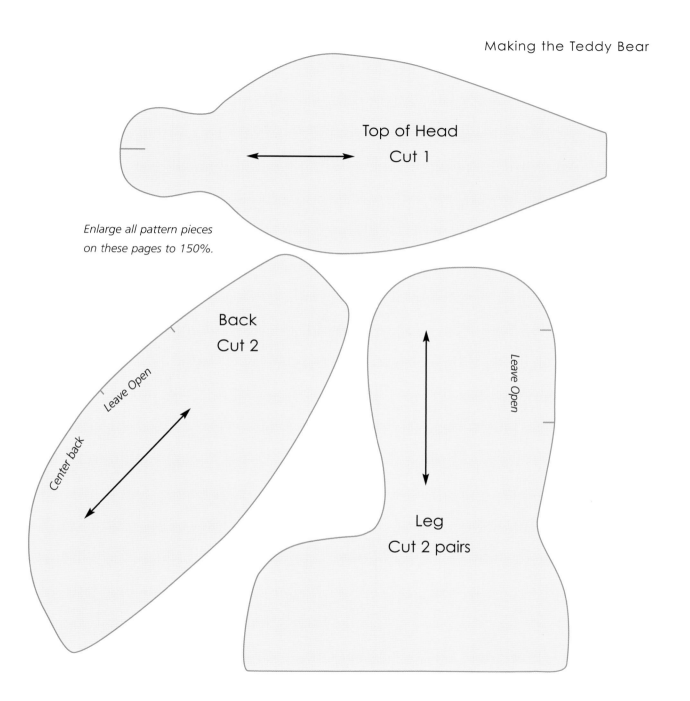

Top of Head
Cut 1

Enlarge all pattern pieces
on these pages to 150%.

Back
Cut 2

Center back

Leave Open

Leg
Cut 2 pairs

Leave Open

# Memory Quilt

A beautifully made quilt signed by your friends and relatives is a wonderful heirloom to treasure all your life. This memory quilt is based on a traditional block design called Hole-in-the-Barn-Door. The center square of each block is unpieced, leaving room for a signature or even a short quotation or message. Be sure to have all writing done with a permanent, waterproof marking pen.

The center squares are quilted in-the-ditch to make the writing stand out. Stippling and a simple leaf border complete the quilting.

Skill Level: Intermediate

# Memory Quilt

## YOU WILL NEED

**For quilt 76 x 65 in. (190 x 162.5 cm)**

Yardage based on 44-in.-(112-cm-) wide fabric with a usable width of 42 in. (106 cm)

- 1 yd. (0.9 m) each of pink leaf print and pink flower print for blocks
- 2 yd. (1.8 m) beige geometric print for blocks
- 2 yd. (1.8 m) green floral print for sashing
- 2 yd. (1.8 m) large rose print for border and binding
- 4½ yd. (4.1 m) small rose print for backing
- Batting, 72 x 90 in. (183 x 229 cm) cotton
- Rotary cutter, quilter's ruler, and cutting mat
- Sewing thread
- Permanent, waterproof marking pen for signatures
- Quilter's pencil
- Quilter's safety pins
- Cotton thread for machine quilting

All measurements include ¼-in. (0.75-cm) seam allowances.

**Pink leaf print**

- Cut 6 strips 3⅞ x 42 in. (10 x 106 cm). Cut strips into 60 squares 3⅞ x 3⅞ in. (10 x 10 cm).

**Beige geometric print**

- Cut 6 strips 3⅞ x 42 in. (10 x 106 cm). Cut strips into 60 squares 3⅞ x 3⅞ in. (10 x 10 cm).
- Cut 10 strips 2 x 42 in. (5.25 x 106 cm).
- Cut 3 strips 3½ x 42 in. (9 x 106 cm). Cut strips into 30 squares 3½ x 3½ in. (9 x 9 cm).

**Pink flower print**

- Cut 10 strips 2 x 42 in. (5.25 x 106 cm).

**Green floral print**

- Cut 7 lengthwise strips 2½ x 57½ in. (6.5 x 144 cm) and 36 lengthwise strips 2½ x 9½ in. (6.5 x 24 cm) for sashing.

**Large rose print**

- Cut 2 lengthwise strips 4½ in. (11.5 cm) wide x length of quilt center, and 2 lengthwise strips 4½ in. (11.5 cm) wide x width of quilt center plus 2 border widths for border.
- Cut 5 lengthwise strips 3 x 61 in. (7.5 x 155 cm) for binding.

**Small rose print**

- Cut 2 pieces 42 x 72 in. (106 x 183 cm) for backing (seamed crosswise).

*Quilt layout*

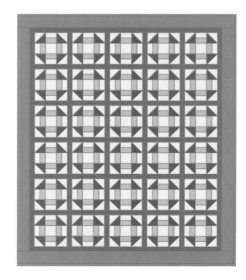

1. From one pink leaf-print square and one beige-print square, make two half-square triangle units. Repeat to make a total of 120 pink leaf/beige half-square triangle units. Press the seam allowances toward the pink leaf-print triangles.

2. With right sides facing, stitch one strip of the pink flower print to one strip of the beige print along a long edge to make a strip set. Press the seam allowances toward the pink flower fabric. Repeat to make a total of 11 strip sets.

3. Crosscut each strip set into 3½-in. (9-cm) segments for a total of 120 pieced pink/beige squares.

4. Ask friends to write a signature or message in the center of each one of the 30 beige print center squares using a permanent marking pen.

*See* Techniques book, page 26, for quick-piecing half-square triangle units; page 24 for making a strip set.

**5** Lay out the units for one block (four half-square triangle units, four two-color squares, and a signed square of the beige print) on your work surface in the correct order. Stitch the units together in three horizontal rows.

**6** Stitch the three horizontal rows together, matching the seams, to form a Hole-in-the-Barn-Door block. Repeat steps 5 and 6 to make a total of 30 blocks.

**8** Stitch a long green floral sashing strip along the bottom of each row of blocks, and another along top of first row. Join rows, aligning vertical sashing strips. Press the seam allowances toward sashing.

**7** Join five Hole-in-the-Barn-Door blocks and six of the short green floral print sashing strips to make one horizontal row of the quilt. Press the seam allowances toward the sashing. Repeat to make a total of six rows.

**9** Measure quilt length through the center. Cut two 4½-in.- (11.5-cm-) wide border strips from large rose print to fit. Stitch them to the sides of the quilt. Press.

*See* Techniques book, page 28, for assembling pieced blocks; page 34, for adding sashing; page 35, for overlapped borders.

## Best Foot Forward

*Use a walking foot when you are machine quilting in-the-ditch and along the border. For the stippling, change to a darning foot and lower the feed dogs.*

**11** Trace the leaf-border quilting design from page 93. Mark it on the border, using a light box and quilter's marker. Join the backing pieces along a long edge. Layer the quilt top with batting and backing, and baste the layers together with quilter's safety pins.

**12** Machine-quilt in-the-ditch around each signed center square. Do stippling across the beige background fabric in each block. Free-motion quilt the leaf design on the borders.

**10** Measure the quilt through the center including the width of two border strips. Cut two 4½-in.- (11.5-cm-) wide border strips from large rose print. Stitch them to quilt top and bottom. Press.

**13** Trim the backing and batting even with the quilt edges. Join the binding strips with diagonal seams into one long strip and press in half with wrong sides facing to make a double-fold binding. Bind the edges of the quilt, mitering the corners.

*See Techniques book, pages 38–42, for quilting techniques; page 43 for making a double-fold binding.*

# Maple Leaf Miniature Quilt

If you haven't got time to piece a bed-size quilt, why not try making a miniature quilt such as this Maple Leaf design? Quick to put together using tiny 1-in. (2.5-cm) patches, it has a special charm of its own and would look delightful as a small wall hanging or decorative table mat.

The foundation method is ideal for dealing with miniature patches, ensuring crisp lines and sharp points. Reduce bulk by using a paper foundation that you can tear away when the stitching is complete.

Skill Level: Intermediate

# Maple Leaf Miniature Quilt

## YOU WILL NEED

**For miniature quilt**
**12½ x 12½ in. (32.5 x 32.5 cm)**

Yardage based on 44-in.-
(112-cm-) wide fabric with
a usable width of 42 in.
(106 cm)

- ⅛ yd. (0.1 m) each of pale-
  green spotted print and
  copper mottled print

- ¼ yd. (0.25 m) dark brown
  textured fabric for sashing
  and binding

- ⅝ yd. (0.6 m) autumn leaf
  print for border and backing

- Tear-away foundation paper

- Batting, 14½ x 14½ in.
  (38 x 38 cm)

- Rotary cutter, quilter's ruler,
  and cutting mat

- Sewing thread and small pair
  of scissors

- 1 skein brown embroidery
  floss

- Quilter's pencil and safety
  pins

- Cotton quilting thread for
  machine quilting

## CUTTING LIST

All measurements include ¼-in.
(0.75-cm) seam allowances.

**Pale-green spotted print**

- Cut patches to fit foundation
  (see page 89, step 2).

**Copper mottled print**

- Cut patches to fit foundation
  (see page 89, step 2).

**Dark brown-textured fabric**

- Cut 2 strips 1 x 3½ in.
  (3 x 9 cm); 3 strips 1 x 7 in.
  (3 x 18 cm); and 2 strips 1 x 8 in.
  (3 x 21 cm) for sashing.

- Cut 2 strips 1 x 42 in.
  (3 x 106 cm) for binding.

**Autumn leaf print**

- Cut 4 strips 2½ x 15 in.
  (6.5 x 38.5 cm) for border.

- Cut 1 piece 14½ x 14½ in.
  (38 x 38 cm) for backing.

**Batting**

- Cut 1 piece 14½ x 14½ in.
  (38 x 38 cm).

1 Using a fine permanent marking
pen and ruler, draw the three
rows of the foundation pattern (shown
full-size opposite) onto the foundation
paper, including all lines and numbers.
This forms one Maple Leaf block. Draw
and number the same foundation
pattern once more, then draw two
more patterns as mirror images. Cut
out around the outer marked lines.

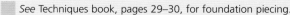
*See* Techniques book, pages 29–30, for foundation piecing.

**2** For the top right-hand Maple Leaf block, piece foundation rows A, B, and C in numerical order, cutting the patches at least ⅜ in. (1 cm) larger all around than the finished size. Repeat for the bottom left-hand block. Then piece the foundations for the two mirror-image blocks.

## Easy-Tear

*Use a short stitch length of about 16 stitches to 1 in. (2.5 cm) on your sewing machine so that the needle perforates the foundation paper at frequent intervals. This makes it easier to tear the paper away.*

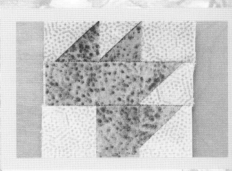

**A**

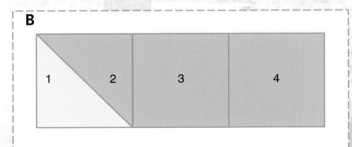

| 1 | 2 | 3 | 4 | 5 |

**B**

| 1 | 2 | 3 | 4 |

**3** Stitch one set of foundations A, B, and C together, matching the seams, to assemble a Maple Leaf block. Repeat to make a total of four Maple Leaf blocks.

**C**

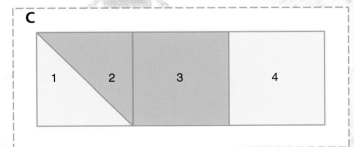

| 1 | 2 | 3 | 4 |

*Foundation Pattern*

*The dotted line shows a ¼-in. seam allowance. For a metric version, draw a 0.75-cm seam allowance.*

**4** Lay out the blocks in the correct order. Join top two blocks into a horizontal row with a short dark brown sashing strip in between. Repeat for bottom two blocks. Press the seam allowances toward sashing.

## Mirror Match

*The Maple Leaf blocks are positioned so that each one is a mirror image of the other. Double-check that you have arranged them in the right order before joining them with the sashing strips.*

**5** Join the two horizontal rows with a dark brown 7-in. (18-cm) sashing strip between them. Press the seam allowances toward sashing. Stitch the other two 7-in. (18-cm) sashing strips along top and bottom.

**6** Stitch the two 8-in. (21-cm) dark brown sashing strips to the sides of the blocks to complete the center panel. Press the seam allowances toward the sashing. Carefully tear away the foundation paper.

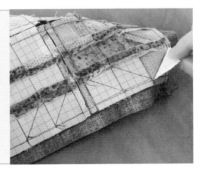

See Techniques book, page 34, for adding sashing.

8 Trace quilting design from page 94. Using a lightbox and a quilter's pencil, trace the quilting design from page 94 onto the borders.

7 Stitch the autumn leaf border strips to the sides of the quilt, mitering the corners. Using three strands of brown embroidery floss, embroider leaf stems in the center squares in stem stitch or back stitch.

9 Layer the quilt top with the batting and backing and baste the three layers together with quilter's safety pins. Machine-quilt in-the-ditch on all the blocks. Free-motion the design on the border.

10 Trim the backing and batting even with the quilt edges. Join the dark brown binding strips with a diagonal seam into one long strip to make a single-fold binding. Bind the edges of the quilt, mitering the corners.

*See* Techniques book, pages 36–37, for borders with mitred corners; page 45 for making a single binding.

# AMISH CUSHION

Project 3 – See page 24

Enlarge the designs to **150**% on a photocopier and trace them onto tracing paper.

Mark Design A on the center panel, Design B on the right-hand green panel and Design C on the right-hand maroon panel, as described in Step 4 of the project.

For the left-hand green and maroon panels, rotate Designs B and C through 180°.

## MEMORY QUILT

Project 11 – See page 80

Mark the design onto the border of the memory quilt as described in Step 11 of the project, repeating it as shown here.

# MAPLE LEAF MINIATURE QUILT

Project 12 – See page 86

Enlarge the design to **200%** on a photocopier and trace it onto tracing paper.

Mark the design centrally onto the border of the miniature quilt as described in Step 8 of the project.

# Index

*All entries refer to Techniques Book unless marked "P"; entries in bold are main entries*